I. SELBORNE: GILBERT WHITE'S VILLAGE

NTIL THE MIDDLE of the nineteenth century, the village of Selborne was extraordinarily remote and inaccessible. When William Cobbett was in the neighbourhood in 1822, he admitted that he had barely heard of it, despite having grown up only ten miles away at Farnham. Selborne was not on the way to anywhere, but was only reached as an end in itself, by means of a long and often arduous diversion from the more frequented routes.

Even on the eve of the Great War, the village street which is now tormented by traffic was rutted and unmade, and quiet enough for animals to graze and for children to walk and play in safety. The road to Alton is a convenience to motorists that dates only from 1847. It replaced a country track that had been worn down by centuries of use and water-erosion into a hollow, sunken lane. The lane was barely eight feet wide, yet in places was up to eighteen feet below the level of the surrounding fields. Travellers along this virtual tunnel saw only a 'narrow stripe of sky and steep banks, almost perpendicular, so near to each other that one carriage cannot pass another except at certain points, and presenting a mass of tangled roots interspersed with shivered rocks'. As Gilbert White had earlier noted, 'these rugged gloomy scenes affright the ladies when they peep down into them from the paths above, and make timid horsemen shudder when they ride along them'. The track was a subterranean one for almost a couple of miles out of Selborne. Initially, it followed a different course from the present road, which has adopted a former footpath. It began as a turning off Gracious Street, just beyond Grange Farm. It then wound its way up the steep hill, passing to the right of Nine Acre Cottage, rejoined the course of the modern road as it ascends to Norton Farm, and eventually emerged into daylight at Hartley Park Farm, where it began a gentle descent into Alton.

For the naturalist, the steep banks of the hollow lane were more of a delight than an inconvenience, particularly because of the 'curious filices [ferns] with which they abound'. The rare green hellebore could also be sought out, and can still, 'in the deep stony lane on the left hand just before the turning to Norton-farm'. It goes without saying, though, that the hollow lane was impenetrable in periods of heavy rain or snow. Travellers to Alton would then be forced to leave the village in a southerly direction, turn westwards into Galley Lane, and, at East Tisted, to join the old Gosport Road that passes through Farringdon and Chawton. The distance to Alton (four miles) was effectively doubled in winter-time.

An equally remarkable hollow lane led eastwards out of the village in the direction of the Forest of Woolmer, but it, too, was generally impassable, and the Forest itself was 'nothing but a hungry, sandy, barren waste'. South of the village, there was at least the road that led by way of Empshott to Liss, though it is still a winding, hilly road, unappealing in olden days to any but the most determined local traffic.

White linked the extraordinary isolation of Selborne with the decline of its medieval Priory. In its hey-day, the convent had been the most impressive complex of buildings between Farnham and Winchester. Far from being isolated, Selborne had been a thriving, populous market town, the regular resort of kings and of other great men. White detected many clues to its former size and prosperity: an unusually large parish church; evidence that the burying ground had once been considerably larger; fragments of ornamental masonry that had been discovered on the north-east side of the village; and the many disused fishponds, a luxury, during the Middle Ages, of the affluent. He deplored the fact that, under the lordship of Magdalen College, Oxford (which lasted more than 450 years), the manor was not 'strictly looked after', its neglect being most evident in the shameful state of its roads.

A curious consequence of Selborne's isolation was the preservation here of manners and customs that had long before died out in other places. Despite the replacement of its early church, the Selborne that White knew seemed, cultur-ally if not physically, to have remained a perfectly preserved Saxon settlement. There were families here bearing Saxon surnames such as Aldred and Kemp. Pure Saxon vocabulary was in daily use (*culver* for pigeon, *ether* for hedge etc.), as were Saxon plurals, such as *housen* instead of houses (*oxen, men, children* and *brethren* being rare examples of this archaic usage with currency today). Not surprisingly, the place-names hereabouts are generally also of Saxon origin, such

SELBORNE

GILBERT WHITE'S VILLAGE
WITH A GUIDE TO HIS HOUSE

by RUPERT WILLOUGHBY

with illustrations by
JULIE ANNE HUDSON

SELBORNE:

GILBERT WHITE'S VILLAGE
WITH A GUIDE TO HIS HOUSE

by RUPERT WILLOUGHBY

SELBORNE IN HAMPSHIRE, a place of 'hollow vales, and hanging woods,' is famed as the life-long home of the Rev. Gilbert White. First published in 1788, White's *Natural History and Antiquities of Selborne* is one of the enduring classics of English literature.

The romantic landscape that inspired White is as rich in human as in natural history. In 1232, a mighty Augustinian Priory was founded here by a warrior-bishop. Though dissolved in 1484, it has left a permanent mark. Crusaders, kings and saints have come and gone. In the 13th century, Selborne nurtured Sir Adam de Gurdon, whose adventures as an outlaw may have inspired the story of Robin Hood. Templar knights lived here quietly and dreamed of Jerusalem.

With the passing of the Priory, Selborne was condemned to centuries of isolation and poverty. Almost completely inaccessible by road, it preserved the aspect, customs and even the speech of an earlier age. A dramatic riot that took place here in 1830, and the construction in 1847 of a new road, marked the ending of its long quietude.

Selborne: Gilbert White's Village tells the story of this remarkable parish from Saxon times. It includes a full account of the author's life, and a detailed description of *The Wakes*, the house in which he lived and worked. It concludes with a step-by-step guide to historic Selborne, pointing out the actual scenes of many of White's observations. It is intended as a souvenir and practical guide for all who come to the village.

as Selborne itself ('sallows brook'), the Hanger (from *hangra*, a steep wooded incline), and the famous Lythes (from '*hlithe*', a slope). Perhaps the most striking survivals are the names of the village green, the *Plestor*, and of Gracious Street. The word 'plestor' would appear to derive from 'plegstow', meaning playplace. Gracious Street, on the other hand, is a corruption of *garscherchestrate*, or 'grass-church street', as in Gracechurch Street in the City of London. Like the vanished St Benet Grass Church in the City, the Priory of Selborne would have maintained a herb garden for medicinal purposes, under the supervision of the *infirmarius*, or brother in charge of the sick. Its location must have been somewhere along Gracious Street, perhaps at Grange Farm.

Where herbal medicines had failed, the traditionally-minded villagers had relied, until relatively modern times, on more dubious cures. White describes 'a row of pollard-ashes' that were to be seen 'in a farm-yard near the middle of this village'. As young trees, they had apparently been 'cleft asunder'. It was explained to him by older people that the trees had indeed been 'severed and held open by wedges, while ruptured children, stripped naked, were pushed through the apertures, under a persuasion that, by such a process, the poor babes would be cured of their infirmity'. By the immediate application of some loam and bandages, the severed trees would usually heal. If not, the operation would be deemed a failure. White's informants swore by the efficacy of the cure, which he considered to be a survival from pagan times. He himself removed two or three such trees from his own garden, one of which, he points out ominously, had failed to heal.

Another curious survival at Selborne was the tradition, once common in England, of virgin *crants*. At the death of a young maiden, special garlands, known as crants, would be prepared for her. These would be carried before the bier and, after the funeral, hung about the church. Each crant was adorned with rosettes and with five paper gauntlets, representing a challenge to anyone who might impugn the honour of the deceased. Despite her 'doubtful' death, the priest in *Hamlet* concedes the honours to Ophelia:

> Yet here she is allowed her virgin crants,
> Her maiden strewments, and the bringing home
> Of bell and burial ...

Once these blameless girls had been buried, the word *Virgin* would usually be appended to their name in the register, the last instance being that of 'Jane Lavington, Virgin', in 1714. However, the custom seems still to have been observed in the lifetime of White (born in 1720), for he had personally witnessed the preparation of such garlands by the wife of the parish clerk, and recalls seeing them hung from the beams in the middle aisle of the church. He adds that in the church of neighbouring Farringdon, which he administered, 'many garlands of this sort still remain'; though the record appears to be held by Abbots Ann, in the north-west of the county, where the custom was still observed in 1939.

The parish registers bear further witness to the conservatism of old Selborne. It is stated that, on 8 October and 11 November 1688, certificates were issued by the vicar (Gilbert White's grandfather) for Mrs Susanna Wakeford and for Stephen Green respectively 'to be touched for the King's evil'. The practice of 'touching for the King's evil' can be traced back to the Middle Ages, and is associated with the popular belief, another survival from pagan times, that 'there's such divinity doth hedge a king'. The kings of England (in imitation of the kings of France) were credited with a power to heal by their mere touch, particularly in respect of scrofula, a disease of the lymphatic glands,. As Herrick puts it in *Hesperides*,

> O Lay that hand on me,
> Adored *Cesar*! and my faith is such,
> I shall be heal'd, if that my King but touch.

Vicar White presumably certificated that the pair were genuine sufferers (for alms were distributed along with the sovereign's blessing), and that they were baptised members of the Church of England. Their timing was perhaps unfortunate, for the country was in the throes of the 'Glorious Revolution' – and the fastidious William of Orange is known to have regarded the practice with some revulsion – but applications of the royal touch were quickly resumed and the popular belief in its efficacy was undiminished. Not many years later, when the infant Samuel Johnson was afflicted, his mother, 'yielding to the superstitious notion, which, it is wonderful to think, prevailed so long in our country, as to the virtue of the regal touch; a notion which our kings encouraged ... carried him to London, where he was actually touched by Queen Anne.' Dr Johnson vividly recalled the encounter in later life, though it seems not in his case to have effected a cure. Unfortunately, the scepticism of his biographer was shared by the Hanoverians – as it no doubt would have been by Gilbert White – and the practice had been abandoned upon the accession of King George I in 1714. It endured in France, however, until 1825.

Another long tradition in Selborne came to an end in only recent times. In 1678, a new vicar, Richard Byfield, contributed forty shillings to the purchase of a clock for the church tower. Although the clock was fitted in 1711 with the latest technology (in the form of a pendulum and anchor escapement), it was necessary for someone daily to climb the two ladders to the top of the tower and to turn its two drums in order to wind up the weights. The Selborne clock was wound in this manner for over 300 years. During the last twenty-eight of those years, it was the responsibility of Mr Bill Andrews of Cobbler Cottage, as it had previously been that of his wife's father and grandfather. Mr Andrews died in 1987, after which the clock was fully restored in his memory and at last fitted with automatic winding gear. The restored clock was set going again by his widow at a dedication ceremony in January 1989. There is no more fitting symbol of the changes that time and technology have wrought on Selborne.

II. GILBERT WHITE AND HIS HOUSE

G ILBERT WHITE'S FAMILY had been settled at Selborne since 1681, the year that his grandfather, also Gilbert, was appointed to the Vicarage. The living was in the gift of Magdalen College, Oxford, and its descent to a junior fellow of that college – White was only thirty – is said to have reflected the 'low estimation' in which it was held.

The elder Gilbert was the son of Sir Sampson White, a native of Cogges, near Witney in Oxfordshire, who had been knighted for his services as Lord Mayor of Oxford. The Whites nevertheless believed, or came to believe, that they were of local origin. They sported the coat of arms (which is much in evidence in the parish church) of the Whites of South Warnborough, about ten miles north of here; though their descent from Robert White, the grantee of these arms in 1514, is unproven. The original grant to Robert is still preserved at the College of Arms: the naturalist would have been interested to know that the three parrots which are prominent in the arms are depicted as Asian rose-ringed parakeets, the 'popinjays' of medieval legend.

The local connections of White's grandmother, who married the vicar within a few years of his appointment, were not in doubt. Rebecca Luckin had grown up at Norehouse in Newton Valence, on the south side of the East Tisted road: her father Robert, a yeoman farmer, had been liable in 1665 for tax on its four hearths. Rebecca bore six children to the vicar. The eldest son, John White, was born in 1688. John became a barrister, though he never established a practice, and later a Justice of the Peace, but appears to have been an unassuming and rather reclusive man, addicted to gardening and the harpsichord. In 1719, he married Anne Holt, daughter of the Rector of Streatham. Their first child, the naturalist, was born in the vicarage at Selborne on 18 July 1720, though his parents had soon taken a house of their own at Compton, near Guildford. Eight children followed in as many years, of whom five – three sons and two daughters – survived to adulthood.

By 1728, when young Gilbert was about seven years old, the family had moved to East Harting in Sussex. A significant change in his life was effected in that year by the death of his grandfather. Old Vicar White, as well as providing handsomely in his will for his parishioners, had acquired a property on the other side of Selborne Street which he had left to his widow. Rebecca was accompanied to her new home by her daughters, Dorothea and Elizabeth, but both girls were married in 1730, one to her father's successor, Mr Cane, the other to her cousin, the Rev. Charles White. Rebecca was not expected to live alone. It was promptly decided that her son John should return to Selborne with his family and that they should share the house with his mother. It was to be the permanent home of Gilbert White, who was nine years old at the time, for the remainder of his life.

The property in question comprised three copyhold tenancies which had been united under the ownership of Henry Wake (1634–1711). The Wakes were a well-to-do yeoman family that had been settled in Selborne since the 1550s. Henry's son, Mark Wake, had given up the tenancy and had moved to Farringdon, where he was in trade as a butcher. The admission of Vicar White in Mark's place is dated 26 April 1716. In the will that the Vicar drew up three years later, he describes the premises as 'my house and orchard in Selborne Street late Wakes'. The naturalist himself always spoke of it as 'the Wakes' or 'Wake's', and the name of that old but obscure Hampshire family has clung to it ever since. Ironically, the house had been known in Henry Wake's day as 'Cooper's', he himself having acquired the core of the property from Richard Cooper, Yeoman, in about 1670.

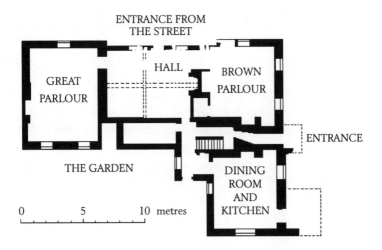

ENTRANCE FROM
THE STREET

GREAT
PARLOUR

HALL

BROWN
PARLOUR

ENTRANCE

THE GARDEN

DINING
ROOM
AND
KITCHEN

0   5   10 metres

The **Wakes** is a fascinating building architecturally because it has 'additions and alterations representing every century from the sixteenth to the twentieth'. The oldest part of the house, much of which still survives, dates from the early 1500s. The original structure was almost certainly timber-framed: the evidence is largely concealed under accretions of plaster, brick and cement. The surviving part of the roof, however, is 'representative of the last throes of medieval carpentry'. The early building consisted of a **Hall** which was open to the roof, with a door onto the Street where there is a **door** today, and probably with an open hearth at one end where there are now a **hearth** and a **chimney**. Behind the hall, on the garden side, was a small **service wing** (now converted into a gentlemen's lavatory) consisting of a larder, buttery and pantry. To the left of it (when viewed from the Street), on the site of the present **Dining-room block**, was a further wing. It contained a ground-floor parlour, with one or more bedrooms above. Access to the upper floor was by a narrow staircase beside the fireplace. The present **ceiling** and **upper floor of the Hall** were inserted in about 1600: by the late Tudor period, open halls of the medieval type had had their day.

The next development was an extension into the garden from the old Parlour unit, thought to have been added by Henry Wake in the 1680s. It consisted of a **kitchen-dining room**, with a raised end, on the ground floor; a *solar* or bedchamber on the floor above; and a **garret chamber** in the roof. The **solar wing** at the Wakes is, incidentally, the only example of its kind in the area. A **stair turret** was constructed in the angle between the new wing and the hall. This was the extent of the house in White's boyhood. It must have been rather cramped, especially after his mother had given birth to another brother and sister. Bedrooms would inevitably have been shared, despite the four-year difference in age between Gilbert and his next brother, Thomas.

White received a certain amount of education from his father, but, from the age of fourteen or fifteen, was privately tutored by the Rev. Dr. Thomas Warton, Vicar of Basingstoke, with whom he boarded. Dr Warton's own sons, a little younger than White, were all brilliant scholars, and one of them was a future Poet Laureate. In 1739, aged nineteen, White went up to Oriel College, Oxford, curiously favouring the college of his uncle Charles over that of his grandfather (Magdalen). Consciously or not, he thereby denied himself any prospect of becoming Vicar of Selborne, for Magdalen, as patron of the living, only ever presented its own men. The university at the time was more of a club than a place of learning, though there were opportunities to study for those who sought them. White also enjoyed an active social life: he celebrated his graduation in 1743 at a cost of eight shillings, quite a considerable sum.

The following year, White was elected to the Fellowship of his college. Residence in term-time was a condition of the award, but the duties were minimal: the purpose of fellowships was as a means of support for the indigent. He pursued a romantic attachment with Hester ('Hecky') Mulso, the sister of his great friend John Mulso, and travelled a good deal, in East Anglia, the Midlands, and the West Country. Long journeys by stage-coach proved a torment, though, as he was prone to travel sickness. A deacon by 1746, he next took up a curacy in his uncle Charles's parish of Swarraton, which obliged him to commute (on horseback) between Oxford and Hampshire. In March 1749, by which time he had given up his rooms at college, he received his ordination to the priesthood.

When his temporary curacy at Swarraton came to an end, White returned to Selborne. With no other work to do, he devoted his time, with increasing passion, to gardening. In 1751, he began to keep a record of his activities in what he called his *Garden Kalendar*. From October of the same year, he was briefly installed in Selborne Vicarage, as temporary curate-in-charge. Still drawn to Oxford, he soon left to take up the office of Junior Proctor at Oriel, and, after his statutory year in office, accepted a succession of curacies in Hampshire and Wiltshire. However, by February 1756 he had returned to The Wakes and had settled there permanently.

It was to be some time before the house became his own. His father died in 1758; but John White had effectively been disinherited by Gilbert's grandfather, who had left The Wakes to his widow and then to his daughter Elizabeth. It had therefore become the property of Elizabeth's widower, Gilbert's uncle Charles.

Without any significant inheritance or the immediate prospect of one, White cherished his now Senior Fellowship of Oriel, and had been delighted in 1757 to accept the Perpetual Curacy of Moreton Pinkney in Northamptonshire, which was in the college's gift. It was to provide him with a modest income for the rest of his life; although, by refusing from the outset to live there, he acquired a bad name at Oriel. The assumption among his fellows was that he was living in idleness on a fortune that he had inherited from his father. Many felt that he was abusing the bounty of the college, by accepting its emoluments when not in genuine need. When, in 1761, he took on the curacy of Farringdon as well, they reviled him as a shameless sinecure pluralist. White was too proud to disabuse his critics by publicising the true state of his finances: his private means actually amounted to a pittance.

Upon the death, in March 1763, of his uncle Charles, he at least came into full possession of The Wakes. The ensuing years were unhappy ones, though, as his prospects of marriage and of clerical preferment seemed both to fade, and his life became one of increasing loneliness and isolation. The study of natural history, an interest since boyhood, was his consolation. In 1767, he began a lively correspondence with Thomas Pennant and the Hon. Daines Barrington, both Fellows of the Royal Society, to whom he had been introduced by his brother Benjamin. (A publisher and bookseller in Fleet Street, Benjamin is described on his tablet in the church as 'a man of great general information and in their researches much consulted by the literary men of his day'. The triptych on wood in the chancel, dating from c. 1510 and attributed to Jan Mostaert, was his gift to the parish.) In an edited form, White's letters to Pennant and Barrington were to be the basis of his *Natural History of Selborne*, the idea of which was conceived in 1771, though it was to be fourteen years in the preparation.

White had other preoccupations in these years. In 1775, he 'dug away forty loads of earth from the end of my kitchen', so that the room was all at one level; and in 1777 he added the spacious **Great Parlour** to the north side of his house, with a doorway into the Hall. Adornments to the new room included 'a flock sattin paper' (light brown with a coloured border), a 'fine stout large Turkey carpet', a 'white and veined Italian marble' chimney-piece (since replaced) and a looking-glass. (The **bay-windows** which overlook the garden date from the early-twentieth century.) The Great Parlour, the *Drawing-room* of a later period, was a fashionable modern comfort, although the early sixteenth-century Hall was to retain, at least for the time being, its function as a common room. Incidentally, White kept 'two basons ... for passion flowers' on either side of the front door, which opened directly into the Hall, but was in a different position to that of today.

The 'old' or 'brown' parlour, on the site of the present **Tea Parlour**, was at times infested with flying ants, but the family seem to have used the panelled upper room of the solar wing, with its fine views across the park to the Hanger, as a drawing room, as well as the master-bedroom of the house. That room, the so-called **solar**, became White's own bedroom and is the room in which he died. His former *bed-chamber*, which faced the Street, and his *study*, with a window overlooking the stable-yard, were above the parlour, in a part of the house that was rebuilt by his brother Benjamin in about 1794. Benjamin's modifications – perhaps opposed in his lifetime by the conservative Gilbert – included the substitution of the former parlour with a **dining-room** (now the Tea Parlour) and the creation of an elegant **bedroom** above. At the same time, Benjamin refaced the **front** of the building in brick.

The common room for the servants was the **kitchen-dining room**, directly beneath the solar, which, following the construction by Benjamin of a new Dining-room, was reduced to the status of a kitchen-scullery. It is a cold and rather gloomy room, as it faces directly onto the part of the garden known as Baker's Hill. The **kitchen floor**, even more low-lying as a result of White's excavations, was stone-paved and tended to 'sweat' during rainstorms. It should be noted, though, that the present floor and hearth are a full half-metre lower than in White's day, having been altered in the 1960s for the purpose of displaying furniture. (The **steps** were, of course, added at that time.) White describes how the hearth would teem with crickets 'after the servants have gone to bed'. He and other family members would presumably have taken their own meals here - often the cooked-up carcases of exotic specimens that had been procured for his examination, such as, on one occasion, a bittern. There was a **window** at the kitchen end, facing onto the garden, and another (now blocked up) at the dining-room end, facing south, with vine-shoots growing outside: White describes how the vine-shoots were once battered by a 'fierce storm of hail'.

Typically, there was no indoor bathroom or lavatory, but White enjoyed the luxury of a 'little-house', or 'necessary', in the garden. Ivy-clad, and screened by strategically-placed elms and laurels, it was perhaps positioned near the **stable** (still standing) that was erected by White himself in 1764, on the south-west side of the house. Before the construction, in about 1910, of the present **service wing**, some sort of screen would have been essential: the 'necessary' would otherwise have been plainly visible from the Street. A nearby border was planted with tulips. The old stable yard now serves as a **Field Study Centre** and **laboratory**. White also built the adjacent **Brewhouse** which is inscribed 'G.W. 1765'.

White had decided, meanwhile, that his treatise on Selborne was to be a true 'parochial history', and should therefore include its antiquities as well as its natural history. The archives of Selborne Priory, which contain much of the early history of the parish, are unusually complete. They were and are still kept in the Founder's Tower at Magdalen, having been recovered from the defunct Priory in 1484. Abstracts of the relevant documents were provided by White's neighbour and friend, Dr Chandler, who was a Fellow of the college. The whole work was to be presented as a collection of letters, based on the genuine, though edited, correspondence of years past with Pennant and Barrington, though as much as half of the total text may consist of 'false' letters which were never actually sent.

In 1776, White hired a fashionable Swiss illustrator, Samuel Hieronymous Grimm, to sketch some scenes of the village. They were to be a notable adornment to the finished work. White's determination to include what his friend Mulso called 'a Farrago of Antiquities' inevitably delayed its publication, and he was sixty-seven years old when, in the autumn of 1787, it finally went to press. In spite of favourable reviews ('a more delightful, or more original work than Mr White's History of Selborne has seldom been published'), it was not an immediate commercial success. The second and third editions were slow to appear, in 1802 and 1813 respectively. The huge popularity and mythic status of the *Natural History* dates from 1830, when an article in praise of it appeared in the *New Monthly Magazine*. The publication of a new edition of the work has since been an almost annual event. Legend has it that it is now the fourth most-published work in the English language, after the Bible, Shakespeare, and *Pilgrim's Progress*.

Its author died at The Wakes on 26 June 1793. At his own request, he was buried simply in the churchyard. He seems to have found peace of mind in his latter years and had led a less lonely life, the house often being filled with relatives including his numerous nephews and nieces, with whom he enjoyed an excellent rapport. Almost until the end, he had been fit enough to carry on with his favourite outdoor pursuits as well as to perform his clerical duties, for he had been curate-in-charge of the parish, in the absence of the Vicar, Dr Taylor, since October 1784. Regrettably, no portrait or description of White survives. It would appear, however, that he was held in great respect and affection by the villagers, who, as his regular suppliers of scientific data, have been described by one writer as the 'collaborators and, in a sense, co-authors' of his book.

As for The Wakes, it was to be occupied by members of White's family until 1839, and in 1844 was sold, by the Rev. Glyd White, to Thomas Bell. A Fellow of the Royal Society, Professor of Zoology at King's College, London, and editor of the highly-regarded 1877 edition of the *Natural History of Selborne*, Bell promptly constructed a much-needed **Library** next to White's Great Parlour. After Bell's death in 1880, the house passed through a succession of hands. Its owner in the early 1890s built an **upper story** above the Great Parlour and Library, which was reached by a new staircase from the hall. The historic core of the house had degenerated by this time into a mere entrance hall. In the early 1900s, the **long corridor** and **entrance porch** were added at the front. There was a further extension to the north, in the rather unfortunate Tudor-revival style, comprising a **billiard-room** (now the museum shop), with a series of **bedrooms** and **dressing-rooms** above.

As for the **garden**, much that White created still survives, including the **fruit wall** for his espaliers, his **sundial**, the **Ha-ha** (one of the earliest in England), and the **brick path** that leads to it. However, his most significant contributions to the landscape are no doubt the **Zig-Zag**, a steep pathway up the Hanger, dug in 1752, on which he collaborated with his brother John, and the **Bostal**, a less exacting thoroughfare but a more considerable feat of engineering, for which White was solely responsible in 1780.

The last private owner of The Wakes died in 1953. A national appeal was launched for funds to purchase the house and endow it as a memorial to White. The bulk of the money was raised from a single donation, part of a trust fund that had been created by Robert Washington Oates in memory of his family. In 1955, the property was formally conveyed to the Trustees of the Oates Memorial Library and the Gilbert White Museum and was opened to the public. The Oates exhibits are displayed in rooms above the Great Parlour, Library and billiard-room (the present **shop**), in the ugly late-nineteenth- and early-twentieth-century extensions. Although the Oates family has no historical connection with Selborne, its members, including the botanist Frank Oates and the Antarctic explorer Captain Lawrence Oates, represent the true spirit of scientific enquiry and are therefore sure to have met with White's approval.

III. CHURCH AND PRIORY

THE HISTORY OF SELBORNE has been shaped by one man more than any other. That man is Peter des Roches. Bishop of Winchester, sometime Justiciar of England, and one of the great figures of his age, Peter founded in 1232 the Priory of the Blessed Virgin Mary of Selborne, as a retreat for fourteen Augustinian canons. During the two and a half centuries of its existence, the convent was to exercise powers of life and death over the inhabitants of Selborne. The social and physical development of the parish, and even aspects of its architecture, were determined in those years. In various ways, the legacy of the Priory is with us still. The impact of one man's whim has been powerful indeed.

Peter was probably a native of Roches-Prémarie-Andillé, near Poitiers, part of the Angevin lordship of Poitou. Though brought up for knighthood, he had served as a clerk in the household of King Richard the Lionheart, and had risen to be Prior of Loches. Recognising his administrative skills, Richard's successor, King John, had introduced him to England in 1200, and had set him to work at the Exchequer. In 1205, through John's influence, he had been appointed Bishop of Winchester.

Between 1208 and 1214, John's defiance of the Pope had brought upon England the curse of an Interdict. The effect of the sentence was that the churches had been closed, their doors literally nailed shut. The clergy had been banned from administering any of the normal comforts of religion, save only 'the baptism of infants and the confession of the dying'. Peter, however, was an uncompromising advocate of royal authority. Alone among the bishops, he had remained loyal to the King, becoming his most trusted henchman. In 1213, his expert management of the royal finances had been recognised by his appointment as Justiciar, the highest executive position beneath the King. The following year, during John's absences in France, he had been the actual ruler of England.

The great table at which the royal dues were collected was covered by a chequered cloth. By shuffling counters around, officials made calculations on the cloth as if it were a giant abacus. The results were recorded on rolls of parchment. Peter, as Justiciar, would sit at one end, facing the sheriff who was presenting his accounts. An anonymous poet had satirised

> The warrior of Winchester, up at the Exchequer,
>> Sharp at accounting, slack at Scripture,
>> Revolving the royal roll ...

The ascendancy of John's Poitevin favourites, of whom Peter was the most prominent, had been bitterly resented by the English. In *Magna Carta*, which the indignant barons had forced the King to sign in 1215 (and of which Peter was a witness), the removal of many of them had been insisted upon. It was nevertheless Peter who had charge of John's son and successor, the boy-king Henry III, and who placed the crown on his head at his coronation.

In 1227, his influence temporarily in decline, Peter had embarked on a Crusade to the Holy Land. He had witnessed the treaty of peace with the Sultan that had been negotiated by the Emperor Frederick II; and had accompanied the Emperor when, on 17 March 1229, he had made his ceremonial entry into Jerusalem. He had returned to Winchester on 1 August 1231, and had entertained the King on Christmas Day. Peter was now an old man: yet the following summer, by a dramatic *coup d'État*, he had ousted the rival justiciar and restored himself to the position he had enjoyed in the reign of John, that of the King's most influential adviser.

If one ambition remained to Peter, it was the salvation of his soul. To this end, he also founded monasteries at Halesowen in Worcestershire and at Netley in Hampshire, as well as, in 1221, the Dominican Friary at Winchester. (For all his worldliness, Peter had been the leading sponsor in England of the newly-formed preaching orders.) He was an extravagant builder (in the Holy Land, he had restored fortresses as well as churches), his projects being as much the self-aggrandising gestures of a powerful man as expressions of piety. Two further foundations were planned on his return, perhaps in fulfilment of a vow, at Titchfield and at Selborne. The latter was conveniently placed, midway between the episcopal seats at Winchester and at Farnham. Moreover, its quarries were already open, and had been supplying stone for the works at Winchester Castle since 1222: remnants of the workings at Selborne can clearly be seen in Hucker's Lane.

Peter bought a site for the new Priory on the soggy south bank of the Oakhanger, about three quarters of a mile from the church. Additional land was acquired by gift or purchase. The King donated about 120 acres in Selborne, and, in a series of charters, accorded various rights and privileges to the Priory, including *furcas*, a power of life and death. The convent was to be responsible for maintaining law and order in the parish: a whipping post and stocks were set up on the Plestor, and a gallows was installed on Galley (*Gallows*) Hill; there was also a ducking stool, the location of which is unknown. The first of King Henry's charters, dated 4 May 1233, marks the formal foundation of the house. Regularly augmented by purchase and by donation, the collective holdings of the Priory at Selborne were eventually to constitute a manorial estate of about a thousand acres, with an equivalent acreage in other parts of the county. In its own manorial courts, held every three weeks, the Priory regulated transactions among its serfs (upon whose labour it could call at any time), and administered justice both civil and criminal. Those lands not farmed or used by the canons themselves (such as the village centre, a sub-manor in itself) were let out to tenants.

Peter was quick to secure possession of the **parish church**, one of three in Hampshire that belonged to the Benedictine Abbey of Mont St Michel. According to *Domesday Book* (1086), where Selborne is first recorded, King Edward the Confessor (1042–1066) had donated the church to its priest, Radfred. He had further endowed him with a 'yardland' (a holding equivalent to that of the average peasant), and had given the rest of the manor to Edith, his Queen.

The parish had enjoyed only brief independence. When the Norman conquerors presented Selborne, Basing and Basingstoke churches to the famous monastery in their homeland, it was to reward them for continually enduring 'the perils of the sea'. During the rectorship of the Abbey of Mont St Michel, the Saxon church at Selborne had been demolished. The **font** is probably all that remains from that building. To quote White, it is 'deep and capacious, and consists of three massy round stones, piled one on another, without the least ornament or sculpture'. On the rim are the remains of the four medieval locks, arranged in diametrically opposite pairs, that secured the wooden cover of the font: there was a risk that the holy water might be stolen by sorcerers. It has been suggested that one of the pairs of locks was added during the Inderdict in the reign of John, to prevent the priest from opening the lid without the approval of a second keyholder. This is improbable, though, as the papal ban had specifically excluded the baptism of infants.

The Saxon church was replaced, in about 1175, by a fine Norman building, still substantially the church of today. Four elegant **arches**, set upon **pillars**, opened on either side of the **nave** into a flanking aisle. These two arcades are still intact; as are the **northerly aisle** and probably the **chancel**, though they are much restored. (The **Tower**, with its mighty walls, has been extensively altered, so its date is uncertain.) The powerful Bishop Peter no doubt easily persuaded the then Abbot to relinquish the three Hampshire churches in his favour, and in 1234 they were added to the endowment of the newly-founded Priory. Selborne church was dedicated, probably simultaneously with the Priory, to the Virgin Mary.

As Rector, it fell upon the Prior to appoint a Vicar. (There were also in the medieval period two outlying 'chapels of ease', at Oakhanger and at Blackmoor, serving the remotest corners of the parish.) He seems never to have considered appointing one of his own community, though each was fully qualified to take services. Under the ownership of the Priory, the church was, however, enlarged, the **south aisle** being extended to approximately its present dimensions. Two side chapels, known as the **North** and **South Chancels**, were constructed at the end of each aisle. All these works date from around the end of the thirteenth century.

The **South Chancel** is thought to have been a private chantry-chapel dedicated to Ela Longespee, the widowed Countess of Warwick. In 1285, she had endowed the Priory with a hundred marks, a considerable sum. According to her directions, one of the canons was to hold the office of chaplain and was to celebrate daily masses for her soul. Gilbert White remembered the medieval parclose, 'an old carved gothic frame-work of timber', which had divided off the chapel. The removal of the parclose in White's youth left a scar on the nearest pillar, above the capital, that is still visible. Countess Ela seems otherwise to have had no connection with Selborne and is buried at Oseney Abbey in Oxfordshire.

Her chapel seems to have served a further purpose, as a burial-place for members of the Order of the Temple. In the thirteenth and early-fourteenth centuries, the Templars had a *preceptory*, or estate, in the parish, in the hamlet of Southington. A pair of graves, one under the north wall of the chapel, the other partly built into the south wall, was discovered in 1877, each containing a perfect male skeleton (though one of the deceased had suffered a broken leg, for which he had received rather inept medical attention). The stone lids to these graves had been removed in the sixteenth or seventeenth century and used as flooring in the North Chancel. Although one of the lids was badly worn, the other was inscribed with a ringed cross at the end of a staff, which White had recognised as the wand of office of the Templars. Three further lids had turned up in the course of the nineteenth century. Two are now affixed to the wall in the former south chantry, close to the graves themselves. Another is displayed in the north aisle.

The **North Chancel**, presumably a chantry too, was similarly divided off by a parclose, the removal of which was also witnessed by White. The once-spacious chapel is today bisected by a new oak **screen** (dedicated in 1949) that honours the dead of the world wars. There are nevertheless many clues to its original appearance. For example, there are traces of red pigment on the outer moulding of the window: according to the fashion in the Middle Ages, the interior of the building was gaudily painted. Its pavement of decorative tiles was carelessly destroyed, presumably when the partitions were removed in the eighteenth century.

Within what is now the memorial chapel, beneath the window, is a shallow, stone-lined grave, presumably that of the founder. Still marked in White's day by 'a very blunt gothic arch on the north wall', the grave was opened up for the first time in his presence, and again in 1948. Besides a few old bones, it was found to be filled with rubble, including fragments of the medieval pavement. The bones included the skeleton of 'a youth or woman', and 'the skull and thigh-bones of a large tall man', a giant, indeed, of at least six foot six inches. They are probably the remains of Sir Adam de Gurdon (who, next to White, is Selborne's most distinguished son) and of one of his wives. Gurdon died around 1305, which is approximately when the North Chancel was built, and is described by a contemporary chronicler, an Augustinian who may have had his information directly from the Priory, as 'giant and warlike'. Gurdon is known to have been a generous benefactor of the Selborne convent, but such directions as he may have given about prayers for his soul are, unfortunately, lost.

IV. THE HAUNTED VALE

THE PRIORY AT SELBORNE was a community of priests, rather than monks, who lived according to the so-called Rule of St Augustine. The Augustinian Canons, or 'Blackfriars', were distinguished by their black lambskin cassocks and their black woollen hoods, which were lined with fur in winter. They also wore white surplices over their cassocks. In theory, the thirteen canons at Selborne and their Prior were required to participate in services throughout the day. Dinner and supper would be consumed silently, to the accompaniment of a reading. The administrative duties allotted to each man, such as the offices of Cellarer, Treasurer and Sacrist, were meant to occupy their remaining time.

In its early days, under the stern eye of its founder and through the example of influential patrons like St Richard of Wich, the ascetic ideal was perhaps to some extent observed. In time, however, the Priory had degenerated into a comfortable billet to which any clever local boy might aspire. The Canons of Selborne lived like lords, waited upon by servants and dining off roast swan and peacock. They had ample time to indulge themselves in hunting, hawking, and even poaching. They enjoyed great wealth without contributing much to its creation, and, indeed, seem to have been negligent and even incompetent land-lords. Their surnames (Holybourne, Odiham, Farnham etc.) reveal them to have been almost invariably local men; often, no doubt, men of humble origin, who had been gentrified by their Holy Orders.

Far from being cut off from temporal affairs, the canons regularly found them-selves at the centre of them. There were visits from great men such as their founder, Bishop Peter, or from royalty, such as Henry III's brother Richard, Earl of Cornwall. King Edward I and his travelling court were entertained here, at considerable expense, on at least two occasions, in 1276 and 1280. (His grandson, Edward III, was to come here too in 1374.) All the while, the wealth of the Priory was constantly being replenished by the endowments of pious laymen. By the death, in 1323, of Prior William de Basing (who once claimed to have been beaten up near Alton by the Rector of Hartley Mauduit), its affairs were nevertheless in disarray. It was not only the finances of the Priory that caused concern: from at least 1357, the discipline of the convent seems to have steadily collapsed.

The subsequent decline of the Priory posed a challenge to successive Bishops of Winchester. The great Bishop William of Wykeham showed a particular concern for its welfare, but his grandmother had been a local girl, the lady Amice de Stratton from Oakhanger. In 1387, Wykeham felt it necessary to make a personal inspection of the delinquent Priory. The outcome of his Visitation was a letter containing thirty-six injunctions, the last of which was that the letter should be read out twice-yearly before the entire convent. The Canons seem to have blithely ignored almost every rule by which they were bound. There was general absenteeism from services. The sacramental vessels were said to be in 'such an uncleanly and disgusting condition as to make the beholders shudder with horror', and the wine that was served in them was sour. The Priory buildings were dilapidated, and the upkeep and administration of the estate had been neglected. Rules of silence were routinely broken. Private reading of the Scriptures was ignored. The canons had even pawned some of the sacred objects in their possession. Some had clearly been more preoccupied with hunting than with the divine offices. Others were absenting themselves for prolonged periods, ostensibly on Priory business. The Bishop even took exception to their appearance. They were dressed up like dandies, in costly furs and gloves, silken girdles, and gaily-coloured boots and stockings. Most shockingly of all, the Canons had been leaving the Priory doors open at night so that it could be frequented by 'disorderly females'. As Bishop William was painfully aware, such misdemeanours were far from unique to Selborne.

Order was only briefly restored. The Priory continued to run up enormous debts (not helped by another royal visit, that of Henry IV, in 1401), which the conscientious Bishop felt obliged to pay off. By 1463, the establishment had been reduced to only four resident canons, each with a personal servant. Their debts were huge, yet they had failed to collect rents from some of their tenants for as much as seven years.

Bishop William Waynflete, the founder, in 1458, of Magdalen College in Oxford, was called in to arrange their affairs. He dedicated himself for twenty-one years to reforming the moribund Priory. Finally, at Waynflete's own prompting, Magdalen applied for the annexation of the Priory and for an appropriation of its property, the college being in dire need of a further endowment. Its application was unopposed, and proceedings for the annexation of Selborne, completed on 24 September 1484, were a foregone conclusion. The sole surviving Canon, Prior Thomas Ashford, was pensioned off: he spent his last years in the Vicarage at Basingstoke. The Priory buildings were already dilapidated, though Magdalen was to support a resident chaplain, charged with celebrating masses for the Priory's benefactors, until 1550. The surrounding land was leased out, and a farmhouse and other buildings had been erected on the south side of the Priory – still the site of **Priory Farm** – by 1526.

The ruins of the Priory itself were to be systematically plundered thereafter. Later in the sixteenth century, cartloads of dressed stone were removed from the site, and resurrected at Andover in the form of the Bell Inn. Further fragments are to be seen in houses all over Selborne, such as most of the old cottages along Gracious Street. Pieces of the fabric continue to turn up in unlikely places, one being discovered only recently, embedded in a bank by the roadside.

The farm-buildings are described in 1526 as a house, two barns, a stable and a dove-house. The present **farmhouse** is thought to have been completed by about 1600, though there are notable additions dating from the eighteenth century. Its early-Tudor forerunner may have been timber-framed: parts of it seem to have been incorporated into the later malmstone structure. Smoke-blackened roof-timbers, evidence of a hall once open to the roof, still survive in the south-facing wing. White was on good terms with Farmer Lassam, the tenant here, a useful source of information about sheep.

The **site of the Priory** is marked today by a few contours on the ground. Much masonry is concealed beneath the surface, however; enough for archaeologists in the 1950s to map the arrangement of the buildings. They probably resembled those at Netley Abbey which are still standing. The central feature was the cloister. This was bounded on the north side, nearest the stream, by the kitchen and refectory, and on the east by the chapter house. The impressive Priory church, south of the cloister, consisted of a nave and a choir with two transepts. The church was about six times the size of the **barn** that now straddles its central point, and more than twice the size of the parish church, which itself is considerably larger than that in any neighbouring village. There were no structures between Winchester and Farnham to compete with these.

While it had existed, the convent had been a constant source of paid employment locally as well as of alms for the poor folk. Gilbert White felt that the presence of the Priory had been a blessing for Selborne, and that its suppression was a setback for the village, which had declined thereafter both in size and prosperity. The subsequent neglect of roads had increased Selborne's isolation: its 'rough and sequestered situation' had given 'a check to resort'. Without the Priory, there seemed to be no incentive for outsiders to frequent the village or its weekly market, of which, by the end of the seventeenth century, there was not even a memory.

Arguably, though, the tenants of the former Prioral lands suffered no adverse effects under the lordship of Magdalen. The college, an impersonal landlord as well as an absentee one, was bound to take even less interest in its distant property than the indolent canons. During White's boyhood, the local agent and rent collector for the college was the aged Jethro Longworth, a man so frail that he could barely write. Moreover, the manorial courts which governed the affairs of the estate had become annual, rather than three-weekly events. The tenants of the manor of Selborne, now termed 'copyholders', were successors to the medieval serfs or *villeins*. They had long ago ceased to owe services for their holdings, but still worked the common fields and enjoyed rights of gathering wood and of grazing their cattle on the Hanger, the High Wood and Dorton. Since the end of the fifteenth century, the common law had intervened to uphold the customs of the manor and to assure them security of tenure. Most had holdings of between ten and twenty acres, though Gilbert White himself had forty and the largest tenant in the manor had seventy-five. On the whole, they benefited from being left to their own devices. Resident squires elsewhere were apt to impose new farming practices and even to remove whole villages in order to create great houses for themselves in secluded parks. The villagers of Selborne were free of such interference.

The historic link with Magdalen was nevertheless to endure until 1967, when the College finally relinquished its freehold of Priory Farm. The manorial courts had persisted until the abolition of copyhold tenure in 1925, meeting, bi-annually at the end, in the old tithe-barn at Grange Farm, and attended by the Bursar of the College if not also by the President himself. It is not known whether these dignitaries enjoyed the feasts, paid for out of the court fees, that were a traditional accompaniment to these occasions. Apart from assuring themselves of their rents, they seem to have been very jealous of their rights to cut down the larger beech-trees for timber, but any departures from 'customary practice' were fiercely resisted. In 1719, the College was successfully sued by the copyholders in the Court of Chancery for encroaching on their rights of common at Selborne. Their involvement with the village was otherwise limited to the periodic appointment of a new Vicar, who was invariably, as in the case of Gilbert White's grandfather, a Magdalen man.

There is a choice of routes to Priory Farm from the village. Behind the church, a footpath through a steep meadow connects with the **Short Lythe** – now a beech-

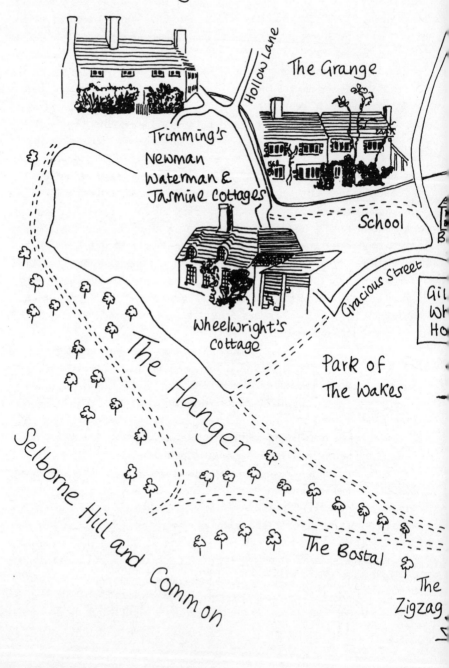

Fisher's Buildings

Hollow Lane

The Grange

Trimming's
Newman
Waterman &
Jasmine Cottages

School

Gracious Street

B

Gil
Wh
Ho

Wheelwright's
Cottage

Park of
The Wakes

The Hanger

Selborne Hill and Common

The Bostal

The
Zigzag

SELBORNE: GILBERT WHITE'S VILLAGE

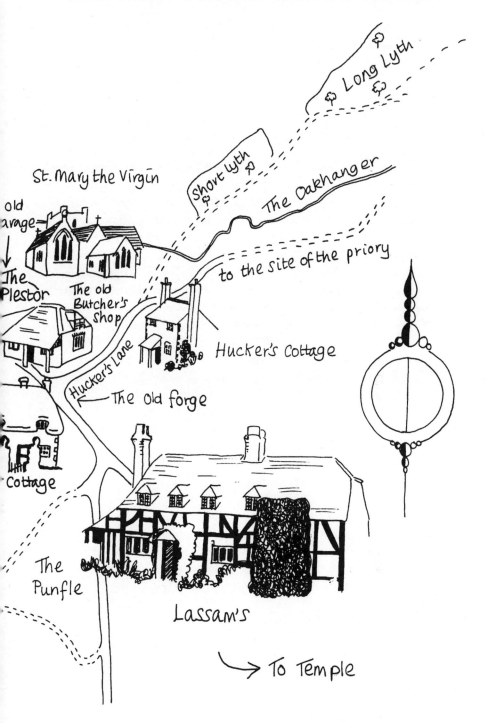

Long Lyth

Short Lyth

St. Mary the Virgin

The Oakhanger

old
vrage

The
Plestor

to the site of the priory

The old
Butcher's
shop

Hucker's Cottage

Hucker's Lane

The old forge

Cottage

The
Punfle

Lassam's

→ To Temple

wood, though White knew it as the rocky pasture where he observed crickets – and the more-substantially wooded **Long Lythe** beyond. Priory Farm, itself on a site known in 1232 as *La Liega*, i.e. Lyth, is further along the picturesque Oakhanger valley, on the opposite bank. The place is reputedly haunted, as White points out in his poem *The Invitation*:

> Still oft at eve belated shepherd swains
> See the cowl'd spectre skim the folded plains.

The alternative route is by **Hucker's Lane**, the narrow entrance to which is just beyond the Queen's Hotel. On the right-hand side of Hucker's Lane is **Dowling's**, the one-time miller's cottage, the mill having formerly stood on the high ground to the rear. As the lane descends, it passes on the same side a gnarled **oak tree** that features in one of Grimm's pictures; the remains of the Selborne **quarry**; and **Hucker's Cottage**, doubtless the smallholding with an adjacent 'lyth' that was owned by a 'John Hukker' in 1437. The lane then merges with the old *Via Canonorum*. This was the Canons' own preferred route, and it has been suggested that it retains, past **Dorton Cottage**, much of its original metalling.

The canons long left a mark elsewhere on the Selborne landscape. On the south-eastern slope of Selborne Hill, beyond the Zig-Zag and the Wishing Stone, is the **King's Field**. Once it was part of the common land, a patchwork of small strips that were apportioned among the tenants. On the south side of the King's Field is a large hillock called **Kite's Hill**. It can clearly be seen from the Liss road in the valley below. Though surrounded by arable land, and for reasons that no one could remember, Kite's Hill was never ploughed, an omission that was reported annually in the proceedings of the manor court. It was even exempted during the Great War from cultivation. Since the adjacent roadway is called **Galley (*Gallows*) Hill**, White deduced that the Priors of Selborne 'might have reserved this little eminence as the place of execution for delinquents'. Such sites were generally chosen with care: the gallows in nearby Chawton was positioned on the ridgeway above the village, where poaching and highway robbery were frequent temptations. Here, in sight of the workers in the common fields and of strangers entering the village, it would have been a constant reminder of the Prior's authority.

V. THE EAGLE AND THE PIKE

THE **ALTAR** *PACE*, or step, of the South Chancel in Selborne Church was originally adorned with tiles, which were subsequently covered over. The tiles were rediscovered in 1877, when the later surface was removed. To these hundred or so medieval tiles have been added those excavated from Gurdon's tomb in the North Chancel, and others recovered in 1953 from the site of the Priory. All the tiles in the church must originally have been supplied by the Priory, as the same patterns are repeated in both locations. In the thirteenth and fourteenth centuries, decorative tiles were affordable only to the wealthy. Often they were rich in heraldic and other symbolism. What stories are told by the Selborne tiles?

A recurring motif is the famous double-headed eagle, recognised throughout Europe as the symbol of imperial power. These tiles probably commemorate the Priory's connection with Richard, Earl of Cornwall. The younger brother of King Henry III, Richard was a magnificent figure in his day. Internationally respected as a statesman, he was elected in 1257 to the throne of Germany, and thereby became emperor-elect, with the title 'King of the Romans'. In England, he was known more conveniently as 'the King of Almayne', a corruption of the French word *Allemagne*. Richard stayed at the Priory, which must by then have been almost complete, in May 1236, at the age of twenty-seven. Peter des Roches was also present: he had known Richard all his life, and the two men may have been travelling together. Like Peter before him, Richard was intent on making a crusade: he had already felled some of his woodland in order to provide for the expedition. The following month, in Winchester, he took the Cross.

Crusades were not undertaken lightly. Four years would pass before he was in a position to fulfil his vow. Richard was eventually to spend seven months in the chaotic Holy Land (1240–1). As the senior Christian prince, he exercised supreme authority there, and won wide respect for his tact and diplomacy. He negotiated some significant territorial concessions, together with the release of Frankish knights who were prisoners of the Sultan. The reputation he had acquired on the Crusade was to stand him in good stead on his return. In operations against the invading French in Poitou, Richard's army was confronted unexpectedly by their superior forces, and threatened with annihilation. Richard decided to negotiate. He had his squire pull off his armour and replace it with the pilgrim's smock that he had worn in the East. Thus attired, and carrying only a staff, he went alone to the enemy camp to parley with the French king. The opposing armies looked on with bated breath. Suddenly, a loud cheer rang out from the French lines. Richard had been recognised by some of the knights whom he had liberated in Palestine. Many now came forward to kneel before him and express their gratitude. The French King, Saint Louis, received him with greater sympathy than he might otherwise have expected, and a truce was agreed, enabling Richard to withdraw his forces to safety under the cover of darkness.

Richard had earlier witnessed the royal charter that had marked the foundation of the Priory, and was one of its most honoured patrons. Richard's arms – still those of the Duchy of Cornwall – consisted of gold *bezants* or coins, a reference, it is said, to his great wealth. In his capacity as 'King of Almayne', these would have been substituted for the double-headed eagle that is depicted on the Selborne tiles. He died in 1272.

A more curious story is told by the tiles that feature a pike. They allude to the most memorable single episode in the whole history of Selborne: the visit to the Priory of St Richard of Wich, Bishop of Chichester, and his performance of a miracle there. Selborne's first Prior, John de Wich, was a close friend of the Saint, both being natives of the town now known as Droitwich. They had been scholars together at Oxford, and later at Paris, and had shared lodgings. They had been so poor that they had had only one complete suit of clothes between them, and had had to take it in turns to go out. Even as a bishop, Richard continued to lead a simple and ascetic life. One day, in about 1250, he arrived to pay a long-awaited visit to the Priory. John was concerned that he had not made adequate provision for his guest. He therefore proposed a visit to the Priory fish-pond. 'My lord, may it please you to go down to the water with us lest perhaps by a gift of God we may be able to catch some fish when you are by?' The Bishop agreed, and a small party went down to the pond. Not only did they fail to net any fish; the net itself became hopelessly tangled, and appeared to be useless. The expedition was on the point of returning home when a friend and relative of the Bishop, Master Nicholas de Wich, made a suggestion. 'Lord,' he said, 'put out your right hand and give a blessing.' He did so, and immediately a pike, at least three feet in length, appeared to hover above the net, as if enticed from the water by the Bishop's gesture. All present believed that they had witnessed a miracle. In 1442, the canons of Selborne still preserved relics of the Saint: a comb, a joint bone, and a pome. The latter was a receptacle shaped like an apple (*pomme*) which, when filled with hot water, was used by priests to warm their hands.

VI. THE HAMPSHIRE ROBIN HOOD

THE FAMOUS SIR ADAM DE GURDON, who is thought to be buried in the North Chancel of the church, was born in about 1220. He inherited an estate at Selborne and East Tisted that had been held by his father and grandfather, both of whom were also called Adam. In return for their land, the family owed the King forty days annual service as men-at-arms. It is possible that they were a branch of the Scottish Gordons who had emigrated to England. According to another theory, the first Adam was a Frenchman, a soldier of fortune who had been encouraged to settle here by King John.

By 1241, the third Adam had succeeded his father as Bailiff of Alton: in other words, he was farmer of the royal lands there. In about 1257, he married Constance de Venuz, the widow, from Newton Valence, of Robert de Pont de l'Arche (a town in Normandy, near Rouen). Her father was Sir John de Venuz, the King's Marshal, and a considerable landowner hereabouts. Sir John, who may have lived at what is now Chapel Farm in Oakhanger, was also the lord of East Worldham. He was entrusted as such with the keepership of Alice Holt and Woolmer, the nearby royal forests. In view of his age, he had promptly handed over these offices to his son-in-law, already knighted, and a trusted servant of the crown.

Gurdon nevertheless took the side of Simon de Montfort, Earl of Leicester, in the baronial rebellion against Henry III. In August 1265, the baronial cause was defeated at the Battle of Evesham. Gurdon, with other rebels, was 'disinherited', their lands being seized by the King and re-distributed among his supporters. It was a measure that generated much bitterness among the rebels. Far from being rehabilitated, many of them, including Gurdon, retreated to the woods and marshes to live as outlaws.

Gurdon had been one of the leading rebels from the south. A tough soldier, renowned for his strength and courage, he had distinguished himself, earlier in the year, by seeing off a Welsh invasion at Dunster. In April 1266, King Henry issued a safe conduct to Gurdon, on condition that he treat for peace. The terms, though generous, appear to have been rejected, despite the intercession at court of a powerful friend, Henry of Almayne – the son of Richard, Earl of Cornwall. In May, Gurdon broke out of Essex and Hertfordshire, and made his way across the Chilterns to Hampshire. In those days, the outlaws in the green-woods were hailed as popular heroes: they were thought to be striking blows for freedom against royal tyranny. Gurdon would have been particularly well received in his own country, where criminal activity had long been regarded as legitimate and even respectable. The precise location of his retreat is not known. One chronicler says it was 'in Alton wood': perhaps this refers to the Pass of Alton, a stretch of the main Winchester road at Chawton that was notorious for highway robberies. Another states that 'he established himself with his followers by the road between Alton and Farnham Castle, in a valley where wooded slopes made it so tortuous as to make it a good place for robbers'. From here, according to the same writer, Gurdon 'raided the countryside, particularly the lands of those who adhered to the royal cause'.

It was left to King Henry's son, the Lord Edward, to defeat the last pockets of the rebellion. More of a statesman than his father, he was prepared to be reconciled with the more useful outlaws; but Gurdon, who had rejected the promise of a safe conduct, had first to be flushed from his lair. Physically impressive (he was over six feet tall), and the equal of any knight in prowess, Edward 'Longshanks' was imbued with the spirit of chivalry, and was known never to resist a challenge. He had the advantage of being some twenty years younger than his adversary. A contemporary writer, relying on sources close to the future king, describes their encounter as follows:

> Adam's strength and prowess were well known and Edward, eager to test them, when he came upon him all ready for a fight, bade his men stand by while he engaged him in single combat. Equally matched they exchanged blows without giving way to each other for some time. At length Edward, who was delighted by the valour and spirit of his adversary, advised him, during a pause in the fighting, to surrender, and promised him his life and fortune. The knight agreed, threw down his arms, and surrendered there and then. Edward gave him the same night to his mother the queen at Guildford with his recommendation; and later, after Adam had been restored to his inheritance, always gave him his affection and confidence.

This writer omits to mention that Gurdon's companions were hanged from the nearest trees, a detail that is recorded elsewhere. The rehabilitation of Gurdon himself is, however, well attested. The royal accounts from January 1267 confirm the restoration of a parcel of land in Alton, which had been entrusted, like Gurdon himself, to the Queen. We read of his reinstatement as *Custos*, or Keeper of Woolmer Forest. He continued to be on call for military duties, too. In 1295, towards the very end of his life, he was one of four knights charged with raising 3,000 able-bodied men in the southern counties to meet a threatened invasion by the French.

Gurdon's encounter with the Lord Edward is chronicled by well-informed contemporaries, from sources at the court or at Selborne Priory. Adapted versions of the tale seem to have passed into folklore. The legend of Robin Hood can be traced to a collection of late-medieval ballads, one of the earliest being the *Littel Geste of Robyn Hode*. Dating from the fifteenth century, it contains remarkable echoes of the Gurdon story. A gallant King Edward pursues the recalcitrant outlaw to his forest lair. Disguised as an abbot, he allows himself to be ambushed. However, he is unusually magnanimous towards his captors, and gives up his money without complaint. When a royal writ is flourished, Robin guilelessly reveals himself to be a faithful subject, though one who has been wronged by corrupt officials. King Edward then identifies himself to Robin, who falls to his knees. The two men are reconciled, and Robin is accepted into the royal service. The Robin Hood legend may well owe much of its circumstantial detail, if not its origins, to the adventures of outlaws like Gurdon, the dispossessed heroes of a popular rebellion, and to other 'merry' criminals who had been harboured in the forests by sympathetic locals.

Gurdon must otherwise have led a fairly peaceful life, one which, fortunately for him, was largely dedicated to sport. In the Middle Ages, hunting was a passion among the nobility, which they, at least, had opportunities to gratify, whether in their own parks or, under licence, in those of the King. The medieval kings were jealous of their forests: the New Forest, Epping Forest and Windsor Great Park are notable survivors of these former royal hunting reserves, which once accounted for as much as a third of the English countryside. It was the duty of men like Gurdon to impose the draconian 'Forest Law' against unlicensed encroachment, including such apparently harmless activities as cutting wood. It would even have been required of the people of Selborne (and in all other places under forest jurisdiction) that their dogs be 'lawed', which meant cutting off three talons from the front paw, minus the pad. Those failing to comply were liable to a hefty three-shilling fine.

The ban on hunting, which affected such a large part of the population, was one of the most oppressive aspects of the medieval monarchy. 'Most men are sportsmen by constitution,' writes Gilbert White, 'and there is such an inherent spirit for hunting in human nature, as scarce any inhibitions can restrain.' Trespasses upon the forest must have been frequent in Gurdon's day. White recalls that, even in his grandfather's generation (late seventeenth century), 'all this country was wild about deer-stealing. Unless he was a *hunter*, as they affected to call themselves, no young person was allowed to be possessed of manhood or gallantry... Our old race of deer-stealers are hardly extinct yet.'

Gurdon, on the other hand, had been licensed from 1253 to hunt throughout the Hampshire forests, provided that he restrict himself to the hare, fox, cat and badger. The licence was granted him for life, and was presumably renewed after

1266, upon his return to favour. Such licensees in fact performed a service to their sovereign, for the animals in question were regarded as harmful to the cherished beasts of the chase. However, in 1272 or 3, during the first year of his reign, Edward I allowed the trusty Gurdon and his wife to enclose a park of their own, apparently at their manor of 'Fowzele' (could this be Foley, near Liphook?), this being a considerable privilege. As Keeper of Woolmer, Gurdon was also charged from time to time with the culling of stags there, or with furnishing the deer or other game that the king might intend for presents: Gurdon himself once received twelve pike from Woolmer with which to stock his fish-pond at Selborne. (According to White, there were 'many vestiges of disused fish-ponds' around the village.) He must have had his work cut out, though, to keep the poachers away.

When Gurdon married Constance, her relative, Sir Thomas Mackerel, had granted them his manor of 'Selborne Mackerel', which was held on a lease from the Priory. The estate included the entire length of the village street with the adjacent plots. During the few remaining years of his life, the Gurdons had paid him a pair of white gloves, worth a penny, in rent. Their tenancy of the Mackerel estate for life had been confirmed by the Prior and Convent in 1262. The couple had applied a few weeks later for permission to build an oratory at their 'court of Selborne that used to belong to Thomas Mackerel': the disposal of such licences in the area was one of the Prior's privileges.

The location of Gurdon's house, or 'court', is a mystery. White thought he had occupied the one-time Templar convent-house in the hamlet of Southington, 'lying about two miles east of the church' – the later 'Temple', where the oratory could still be seen. Joan, Gurdon's sole daughter and heiress, married Robert Achard. She is known to have been a generous benefactress of the Priory, to have moved away from the area, and to have been still alive in 1319. White speculated that, as a further act of piety, Joan had donated her father's house to the Knights Templar in her lifetime. (They would barely have had time to enjoy it: the Order of the Temple was dissolved in 1312.) However, a document from the Priory archives firmly locates the Knights at Southington by about 1260, when Gurdon's career was at its height. Moreover, the old manor-house where he had lived was still being referred to in 1353 as the 'court of Gurdon': a document from that year describes the tithes and other payments that are to be collected there. As a preceptory, Temple Farm was exempt from such dues, a privilege which it would continue to enjoy until the end of the nineteenth century. The theory that Gurdon lived at Temple must therefore be rejected.

The 'court of Gurdon' is more likely to have been on the south-east side of the Plestor, extending into the present churchyard. As White himself relates,

Gurdon and his wife had, in 1271, renounced all their rights in the Plestor to the Priory. At the same time, however,

> Gurdon reserved to himself, and his heirs, a way through the said Plestor to a tenement and some crofts at the upper end, abutting on the south side of the church-yard. This was, in old days, the manerial house of the street manor, though now a poor cottage; and is known at present by the modern name of Elliot's.

Manor-house and church were thus perched side by side on the top of a steep mound that is remarkable for its natural defences – an ideal situation for a chiefly abode. The word 'court' (*curia*) implies a complex of buildings around a central courtyard: 'Elliot's' was, presumably, the sole survivor. Since demolished, it is shown in Grimm's pictures to have stood approximately at the entrance to the present Vicarage (built in the 1970s in a former coalyard). It is to all appearances a humble, unprepossessing abode, though with a high roof suggesting that it may have been of the 'open hall' type. There was evidently no trace in White's day of an oratory. It is only surprising that one was required here, given the proximity of the parish church. The Prior who licensed it to the Gurdons may have had his own reservations, for their attending the mother church at Christmas and on all other major feast days had been insisted upon.

Wherever it was, we may imagine that Gurdon's house, like that of another traditional squire, was 'not so neatly kept as to shame him or his dirty shoes, the great hall strewed with marrow bones, full of hawks' perches, hounds, spaniels, and terriers, the upper sides of the hall hung with the fox-skins of this and the last year's skinning ...' With his retainers to keep him company and to share his accommodation, the household presided over by Gurdon was no doubt a boisterous one. The memory of him at nearby Hawkley is as a ruffian, who expropriated the village mill from the Bishop of Winchester, but was forced by King Edward to return it. He was further obliged to restore to the Bishop, and to his tenants at Farnham, their age-old rights of pasture in Woolmer, which for some reason he had denied them. Gurdon had no doubt adapted very easily to his career in crime.

He would hardly have been best-known for his pious pursuits: in the early 1290s, Constance having died, he nevertheless arranged a gift to the Priory of eight acres in Oakhanger, to assure himself of their prayers. He probably lived into his eighties, and was dead by 1305, when a second wife, Agnes, is described as his widow. If the 'North Chancel' of the parish church was indeed a chantry-chapel, founded by Gurdon for the good of his soul, the great skull and thigh-bones rediscovered there in 1948 are almost certainly his. The extra inches would have helped to equal the odds in his battle with King Edward.

VII. THE KNIGHTS TEMPLAR

W HITE WRITES OF THE KNIGHTS TEMPLAR, whose coffin-lids in the parish church so fascinated him, that they 'had considerable property in Selborne; and also a preceptory at Sudington, now called Southington, a hamlet lying one mile to the east of the village'. The convent building, reduced to a 'mean farm-house', was all that remained, although another farmhouse had stood 'in the memory of man'. It is remarkable that, in 1665, the tithing had been credited for tax purposes with no less than eighteen separate households; yet they had inexplicably disappeared within the space of a hundred years, leaving only the converted convent-house. Still known as Temple, that building was substantially altered and extended in the early nineteenth century, and made into a residence fit for a gentleman. Fortunately, though, the original building had been carefully recorded by White and his illustrator in the *Antiquities*:

The middle part is an hall twenty-seven feet in length, and nineteen feet in breadth; and has been formerly open to the top, but there is now a floor above it, and also a chimney in the western wall. The roofing consists of strong massive rafter work ornamented with carved roses. I have often looked for the lamb and flag, the arms of the knights Templars, without success; but in one corner found a fox with a goose on his back, so coarsely executed, that it required some attention to make out the device.

Beyond the hall to the north is a small parlour with a vast heavy stone chimney-piece; and, at the end of all, the chapel or oratory, whose massive thick walls, and narrow windows at once bespeak great antiquity. This room is only sixteen feet by sixteen feet eight inches; and full seventeen feet nine inches in height. The ceiling is formed of vast joists, placed only five or six inches apart. Modern delicacy would not much approve of such a place of worship: for it has at present much more the appearance of a dungeon than of a room fit for the reception of people of condition... The field on which this oratory abuts is still called Chapel-field. The situation of this house is very particular, for it stands upon the immediate verge of a steep abrupt hill.

The name of this place is ultimately derived from the Temple area of Jerusalem where the Knights had had their first headquarters. (The Aqsa mosque on the Temple Mount, where they were accommodated, was thought to be the former Palace of Solomon.) Founded by a French knight who had participated in the First Crusade, the Templars had developed after 1118 as an order of militant monks, dedicated to protecting the pilgrim routes to the Holy Land. With their sister order, the Knights of St John or 'Hospitallers', they had grown into an efficient, regular army, crucial to the defence of the crusader states. At the same time, both orders had acquired extensive properties in the West, which were often the endowments of pious laymen. In control of vast wealth and assets, bankers to the kings of both England and France, the Templars had become an international corporation, with, during the thirteenth century, as many as 7,000 members. Their estates were known as 'preceptories' (those of the Hospitallers were called 'commanderies'), and were exempted by the Pope, to whom they owed their sole allegiance, from the payment of tithes. It was intended that any surplus resources should be sent instead to the Holy Land.

The membership consisted of knights (who were men of noble birth), sergeants (their inferiors in rank), and clerics (the chaplains of the Order, who performed no military duties). The characteristic Templar tunic, white for the knights and black for the sergeants, was embroidered with a red cross. This was worn on active service over the *hauberk*, or tunic of mail. When the crusaders were driven out of the Holy Land in 1291, the Templars were the last to board the ships. By that time, however, many members of the Order had never even been to the East. There is evidence of men being recruited who were beyond military age, solely for the skills that they could apply in the preceptories.

In contrast to the Augustinians and other monastic orders, who were notorious for their moral laxity, the Templars were bound by strict rules of conduct and were renowned for their probity. For example, the brothers were not permitted to carry money without permission. If a brother died and was found to have unauthorised money in his possession, he would be denied Christian burial: it would be assumed that he had stolen it.

Widely suspected of being a secret cult and of serving their own interests, the Templars were inevitably open to charges of hypocrisy. At dawn on 13 October

1307, on the orders of King Philip IV, all Templars in France were suddenly arrested. They were collectively charged with an implausible catalogue of 'abominable crimes', ranging from sodomy to devil-worship. Confessions were extracted under torture, although many of these confessions were subsequently retracted. Arrests of the Templars throughout Christendom followed swiftly, by command of the doubtful Pope. By 1312, he had been persuaded to suppress the Order entirely. The obsessively religious King Philip may well have believed in their guilt, although, in view of their considerable wealth and property and his own huge debts, he must also have been impelled by a strong financial motive.

In March 1314, leading French Templars, including the elderly Grand Master, Jacques de Molay, were burned at the stake in Paris for their alleged heresy. Before going to his execution, Brother Jacques proclaimed a spirited defence of the Order. He said that there had been no churches or chapels anywhere, apart from cathedral churches, that had been better kept and adorned than those of the Order, or where the divine services had been more assiduously observed. Nor was there any other order which had given alms more generously, for the Templars had given alms thrice-weekly to all comers. Finally, he stated that he knew of no order or nation that had given more of its blood in the defence of Christ. As the flames consumed him, he uttered a terrible prophesy. He declared that, within the year, both the Pope and King Philip would answer before God for their crimes. His prophesy was fulfilled: both men died soon afterwards.

Exchanges between the Templars and the Priors of Selborne are documented from the middle of the thirteenth century, when Brother Richard Carpenter was preceptor. They had settled at Southington by at least 1260. The size of their establishment at Selborne is not known. Apart from the *preceptor*, or administrator, there may have been a chaplain, an almoner, a marshal and a steward. The five stone coffin lids discovered in the church presumably date from the late-thirteenth or early fourteenth century, when the building was extended. If all the tombs were of Templars, the mortality rate at Southington during that short period was relatively high.

The fate of the last Selborne Templars is not recorded. They may have ended their lives in prison, or as pensioners. It is hard to think of heretical initiation ceremonies being carried on here. They may simply have been transformed into Augustinians and sent to the Selborne Priory, where, to judge from experiences elsewhere, they would not have been particularly welcome.

On 2 May 1312, the Templar property was granted, almost in its entirety, to the Knights of St John. The Hospitallers seem not to have occupied their estate at Selborne, but to have let it out to tenants. Temple Southington nevertheless remained in their possession until the Dissolution of the Monasteries in the reign of Henry VIII, when all the Order's property in England was confiscated. The estate subsequently passed into the Seymour and Norton families. In the seventeenth and eighteenth centuries it changed hands many times, and in the nineteenth it belonged to Sir Archibald Keppel Macdonald, Bart. It was he who sold it, in 1865, to the then Attorney-General, and future Lord Chancellor, Sir Roundell Palmer, who at the same time purchased the Blackmoor estate in the valley below. Pious and scholarly, Palmer was elevated to the peerage as a baron in 1872, and in 1882 was created Earl of Selborne and Viscount Wolmer. Lord Selborne employed Alfred Waterhouse on the construction of a grand residence and model village at Blackmoor. Discomfited by the exemption from tithes still enjoyed by his farm at Temple (as Lord Chancellor, he sponsored legislation which enforced their payment by nonconformists), he conscientiously arranged for the reversal of this rather quaint historical anomaly: Temple's medieval status as a preceptory had never been formally revoked.

'Not many years since,' writes White, 'this place was used for an hop-kiln, and was divided into two stories by a loft, part of which remains at present, and makes it convenient for peat and turf, with which it is stowed.' Any memory of such indignities was obliterated by the gentleman-farmer who converted the house in the early nineteenth century. The moderately-pitched roof and elegant Georgian Gothic window-frames that are his legacy date the works to around 1820. Unfortunately, almost all the features described by White were discarded in the process.

Temple has been further transformed since 1865, the house having been progressively expanded and modernised under the ownership of the Palmers. There remains little visible evidence of its medieval origins. The hall, its dimensions so carefully documented by White, survives under a modern roof, and is used as a kitchen. Its thick malmstone walls are largely intact, and, on the western side of the house, are exposed. Some of the adjacent parlour may also survive; the Chapel which lay beyond it is but a memory, the site being occupied today by a terrace.

Temple Manor continued to be occupied by tenants until 1936, when the third Lord Selborne moved here with his family. Since 1972, Blackmoor House has been divided into flats, whilst Temple is today the country residence of the fourth Earl of Selborne and his Countess. A magnificent garden has been created on the former farmland at the back of the house. Still more impressive are the views over Blackmoor and the Forest of Woolmer. The house and garden are not, however, open to visitors, and no view of them is to be had from the boundaries.

The old parsonage, birthplace of Gilbert White

VIII. 'WE ABOUND WITH POOR'

ALMOST OPPOSITE THE WAKES is the village green, **THE PLESTOR**, 'play-place' for the youth of Selborne since medieval times. It was much to the credit of their ancestors, writes White, that they 'thought proper to assign so spacious a spot for the sports and amusements of its young people'. The Plestor must have been a great convenience in his day: as he notes elsewhere, 'the parish swarms with children'. In Grimm's illustration of the Plestor (1776), a couple of them can be seen enjoying a game of cricket. The village maypole is also shown, on the centre of the green. White records that it was blown down in a great storm on New Year's Day 1779, but was resurrected, with a fresh coat of paint, the following spring. An earlier storm, in 1703, had done for a 'vast oak', with seats around its base, whose branches had covered almost the entire area of the Plestor. This 'venerable tree' had been 'the delight of young and old, and a place of much resort in summer evenings; where the former sat in grave debate, while the latter frolicked and danced before them'. In White's time there was only one tree on the Plestor, an ash, described as 'vast' and 'a huge, stubborn mass'. According to Grimm's picture, it stood at the top of the green. That position is now occupied by an **oak**, planted in 1897 in honour of Queen Victoria's Diamond Jubilee, whilst the large **sycamore**, nearer the Street, was planted by White's brother.

The Plestor had also been the scene of Selborne's bustling weekly market and of its annual fair, held on three days in August, which had been permitted under royal charter in 1270. It is no coincidence that the Gurdons had made the site over to the Priory in 1271, an act of civic generosity as much as of piety. Neither market nor fair seems to have survived the hey-day of the Priory. More durable relics of those days were the stocks and whipping-post, which, according to Grimm's picture, were at the top end of the Plestor, to the right of the entrance to the churchyard. (An earlier stocks having been stolen in 1750, the parish had offered a reward of two guineas to anyone revealing the culprit.) Presumably these instruments remained here until the abolition of public executions in 1868.

The great **yew-tree** beside the church – prominent in Grimm's picture and a notable landmark within living memory – is no more. When White was writing, the measurement of the yew-tree, which he considered to be as old as the church, was 'twenty-three feet in the girth', with 'an head of suitable extent in its bulk'. The girth of the tree in 1981 measured nearly twenty-six feet and it had grown to such a height – some sixty feet – that it dwarfed the church. Unfortunately, on 25 January 1990, it was completely uprooted and toppled in a terrible storm. Nearly thirty Christian burials, dating back to about 1200 A.D., were discovered in the crater. The oldest and deepest coffin had been placed directly against the south side of the yew, which is thought at that time to have been about three feet in diameter. The trunk of the tree, severely pruned, was replanted in the vain hope that it would recover. It lives on, however, through a cutting taken at the time of the fall, which was replanted in November 1992, opposite the church door. According to an expert, the father-tree was some 1,400 years old. The church may well have been founded in the seventh-century by the earliest Saxon converts, and the yew planted at the same time.

As for the buildings that surround the Plestor, many would be recognisable to White, but a notable loss is the parsonage (on the west side of the church) in which he was born. The present **OLD VICARAGE** was built on the site in 1842. Fortunately there are several views by Grimm of the previous building and a detailed description of it in *The Antiquities*, which suggest that it was a timber-framed structure, a hall with cross-wings at each end, that would have been erected almost certainly before 1500. The Vicarage when White knew it was 'an old, but roomy and convenient edifice. It faces very agreeably to the morning sun, and is divided from the village by a neat and cheerful court.' Its hall had originally been open to the roof, until a modernising vicar (presumably an Elizabethan) had 'flung a floor across, and, by partitions, divided the space into chambers. In this hall we remember a date, some time in the reign of Elizabeth; it was over the door that leads to the stairs.'

It was from here that Vicar John Longworth was ejected in favour of a Puritan during the Commonwealth, retiring 'to a little tenement about one hundred and fifty yards from the church, where he earned a small pittance by the practice of physic'. The property to which White refers was the one next along from his own, now called **COBBLER COTTAGE**. Longworth's holding, inherited by his wife Ann in 1678, comprised a total of 47 acres in scattered strips. Restored to the benefice in 1660 (and liable for tax on the Vicarage's eight hearths in 1665), Longworth had administered the parish until his death. His elder son John, baptised in 1640, was no doubt the 'Mister Longworth', assessed with a comfortable five hearths in 1665; whilst a younger son Jethro (1648–1736) was the decrepit agent for Magdalen College in White's youth.

Vicar Longworth is said to have been 'so impoverished by his misfortunes, that he left the vicarage-house and premises in a very abject and dilapidated state'. Soon after his own appointment in 1681, White's grandfather had 'floored and wainscoted the parlour and hall, which before were paved with stone, and had naked walls; he enlarged the kitchen and brewhouse, and dug a cellar and well: he also built a large new barn in the lower yard, removed the hovels in the front court, which he laid out in walks and borders; and entirely planned the back garden, before a rude field with a stone-pit in the midst of it.' His son-in-law and successor in 1727, Mr Cane, 'new built the back front' of the house, whilst Mr Etty, vicar from 1758, re-roofed it. (The cellars and domestic buildings at the west end of the house seem to have survived the rebuild of 1842.) White noted that human bones had often been dug up in the court and garden of the Vicarage, the churchyard having once been more extensive. He confesses in his poem *The Invitation* to being greatly attached to his birthplace, and 'smit with its beauties' from an early age.

Another building that has disappeared since White's day is the cottage called *Elliot's* (on the top right-hand side of the Plestor when viewed from the Street), a remnant of the Gurdon manor-house. Other buildings around the Plestor are just as White knew them. The **GALLERY OF THE ASSOCIATION OF MOUTH AND FOOT PAINTING ARTISTS**, despite its new frontage, was then kept as a general store by John Burbey. He had acquired the property from Thomas Lumbell in 1774. Burbey's stock included herbal medicines, such as 'red bark' which was prescribed for the ague. He was one of White's closest friends in the village, and shared his enthusiasm for natural history. At one time he kept a brown owl, a 'great washer', which unfortunately drowned itself in a water-butt. In 1792 there were no less than eleven house-martins' nests under his eaves. In 1779 White writes of an attempted break-in whilst Burbey slept upstairs. The assailants, bent on plundering the till, were apparently disturbed whilst attempting to force an entry through the shuttered windows. It was here that Timothy the tortoise, White's famous 'sorrowful reptile', was periodically weighed, 'to the great-diversion of the shop-keeper's children'. Burbey also described how a sleep-walker had once launched himself from the first-floor window, suffering no more than a slight cut. Further excitement is recorded by a puzzled naturalist in January 1787: 'This afternoon I saw at the house of my neighbour Mr Burbey, 54 young girls, which he entertained with tea, & cakes: they were, except a few, natives of the village.' The Maxwell family, originally from Harting in Sussex, ran the shop from 1832 to 1948.

From 1786, Burbey had had to put up with a rival business on the opposite side of the green: White reports that 'John Carpenter has opened a shop with a great bow-window to the Plestor, in which he sells ironmongery, hardware, cheese and breeches'. He also dealt in peat: White had three loads delivered in December 1790 at a cost of nine shillings. Carpenter's house, **PLESTOR COTTAGE**, has now been converted into two separate dwellings and at one time was divided into three. The bay window has gone, but appears in a nineteenth-century photograph, at the street-end. Carpenter was also the village carpenter, and had worked occasionally for White, notably on a figure of Hercules for his outer garden. An entry in the *Garden Kalendar* places his workshop at the back of the house. 'At two o'clock in the shortest days the shades of my kitchen & hall chimnies fall just on the middle of J. Carpenter's workshop,' he writes. There is no trace of such a building today.

One of White's nearest neighbours was John Hale, Yeoman – also the village butcher, and White's cousin on the Luckin side. Hale was another of White's intimates: he and Burbey were the two witnesses to his will. He occupied the large house on the corner, **PLESTOR HOUSE**, which dates approximately from the seventeenth century. There had probably been a medieval hall-house on the site, for smoke-blackened rafters have been re-used in the roof of the present malmstone building. It was in Hale's time – he acquired the property in 1763 – that the mortar was ornamented with pieces of iron ore from Woolmer Forest (or, as White puts it, 'studded with tenpenny nails'), a local peculiarity known as 'garnetting'. The present street-front dates from 1796, after White's death. Since he directly overlooked the adjacent **BUTCHER'S SHOP** (with its attendant 'blood and filth'), he had persuaded Hale to let him plant four **lime trees**, two of which survive, as a screen. He had an account with Hale and paid his bill annually – about £33.

The butcher's shop, which closed for business as recently as 1911, was the first in a row of tradesmen's workshops. That of John Carpenter, behind his house on the Plestor, would probably have been accessible from the Street. Next, on the site of **THE LIMES**, were the premises of George Tanner, a saddler and shoemaker. Tanner, as well as supplying his products to White, reported to him on the movements of birds (as did his son Will) and tasted his home-brewed beer. Was his perhaps the 'straight cottage chimney' under which White crouched one summer to observe the antics of swallows, which dived so low through the shaft that he feared his eyes might be pecked out? Tanner's cottage was neat but decrepit, with low ceilings and a thatched roof. It appears in a photograph of 1900, but gave way soon afterwards to the present villa.

Further along, past **White's Cottage**, is **THE QUEEN'S HOTEL**. It was resurrected in 1837 on the site of an earlier alehouse, *The Compasses*, which is documented from at least 1600. White describes a memorable wedding party that took place here in 1783. The original building (only part of the back wall survives) was destroyed by an arsonist in 1830.

Past the Queen's Hotel, on the farther side of Hucker's Lane, is the former **FORGE**, said to be five hundred years old, and a working smithy until 1969. The last smith to own it was Clifford Tarr. According to a *Garden Kalendar* entry from 1762, the house of Boxall the blacksmith was seventy yards from the butcher's shop. It was taken over in 1774 by John Lassam.

'We abound with poor,' writes White; 'many of whom are sober and industrious, and live comfortably in good stone and brick cottages, which are glazed, and have chambers above stairs; mud buildings we have none.' Glass had not always been affordable to cottage-dwellers. **LASSAM'S**, on the west side of the Street, beyond **The Selborne Arms** and the **footpath** to the Hanger, was occupied by generations of the Lassam family. White immortalises John Lassam as a useful grafter of roses. The small Tudor **lean-to** at the southern end of Lassam's cottage, a former pantry, retains its original wooden mullions, only having been glazed in the last fifty years. Candles were another luxury beyond the reach of the villagers, who instead burned rushes, dipped in grease. These rush lamps, prepared by 'decayed labourers, women and children', were an efficient alternative, according to White, as they were slow to burn and gave a 'good clear light'.

Other typically solid cottages are to be seen in **GRACIOUS STREET**, the entrance to which is opposite the Plestor. One of the most interesting is **WHEELWRIGHT'S COTTAGE**, far down on the left-hand side, beyond the sharp turn to the right. Probably of Tudor origin, it was substantially altered in 1697. The adjacent **smithy**, closed in 1943, may well have supplied the thirteenth century ironwork on the church door. White often refers to its owner, Peter Wells, and to his well, which tended to overflow after prolonged rain. The house was converted into a pair of labourer's cottages in the nineteenth century, when it acquired an additional staircase, but has since been restored to a single, highly-desirable dwelling.

A little beyond on the right, directly opposite **Newman**, **Waterman** and **Jasmine Cottages**, is the site of a former pond, now a **parking space**. This was doubtless the pond to which White refers in his journal on 1 February 1785: 'On this cold day about noon a bat was flying round Gracious street pond, & dipping down & sipping the water, like swallows, as it flew: all the while the wind was very sharp, & the boys were standing on the ice!'

The Tudor cottage at the far end of Gracious Street, **TRIMMING'S**, is unchanged, though, and still bears the name of its eighteenth-century owners. Will Trimming, often mentioned by White, took over from his father in 1780. On the opposite side of the road is **THE GRANGE**. It was here that the Prior of Selborne, as Rector, would store the tithes that he had collected from his parishioners. Originally a tenth of all the produce of the land, payments were later accepted in the form of money. A portion of these dues was passed on to the vicar. There is evidence that the Grange was rebuilt in around 1420. However, all that remains of the medieval farmhouse, which was timber-framed, is part of its roof. As at Plestor House, smoke-blackened timbers have been recycled in the later structure, which probably dates from around 1600. The Grange was further extended and modernised in about 1700, for White had 'conversed with very ancient people who remembered the old original Grange'. The improvements of that time included a Jacobean-style staircase. During the lordship of Magdalen, the annual (later bi-annual) manorial courts would assemble here, in a great wheat-barn that is now no more.

Beyond is a track leading to the **HOLLOW LANE** that was once the main road to Alton. At this end it has hardly changed since the eighteenth century. For example, the wall lettuce, male and hart's-tongue ferns that White observed on 30 October 1765 'in a most shady part of the hollow lane under the cover of the rock as you first enter the lane in great plenty, on the right hand before you come to nine-acre lane', can be found in the very same place today.

Opposite Grange Farm, in the angle between **Northfield Hill** (the Newton Valence Road) on the right and the lane leading to the Hanger on the left, are **FISHER'S BUILDINGS**, completed in the early eighteenth-century. Now divided into four dwellings, they seem to have started off as a single, timber-framed farmhouse: there is evidence that the wing abutting Northfield Hill was once a stable. It was the property of James Knight, another of White's friends and collaborators. Farmer Knight, whose grand relatives were lords of Chawton, also owned the **ponds** beyond (in the garden of the present **Coneycroft House**), the former manorial stews, in whose wild-life White took a keen interest: he would pass this way regularly on his journeys to and from Farringdon. In 1780, Knight leased the farmhouse to the parish for conversion into a workhouse, a then novel response to the challenge of providing for paupers. He sold the freehold in 1794 for the sum of £250, and Fisher's Buildings served as a poorhouse until 1835.

As a disincentive to fecklessness, the workhouse regime was deliberately tough (for example, the sexes were forced to live apart), and that at Selborne was as cheerless as any. After the Napoleonic Wars, rural England was in crisis, not helped by the heavy demands on farmers to meet their tithes, the value of these dues having been fixed in more prosperous times. They were unable as a result to pay their workers a satisfactory wage. When Cobbett visited the village in 1823, a local told him that 'he did not believe there was a more unhappy place in England... there's always quarrels of some sort going on ... on matters of rates and tithes mostly'. Not long before, a shot had been fired through the Vicar's window.

Discontent among the labouring classes came to a head in 1830, following a succession of poor harvests. Violent demonstrations throughout the country were thought to have been organised by a mysterious 'Captain Swing'. On Monday 22 November, about 400 labourers, some armed with clubs, assembled at Selborne and took out their frustrations on the Vicar and on the guardian of the workhouse, both of whom were deeply unpopular. The Rev. William Rust Cobbold, described as 'a very corpulent man', was a supercilious bully, who seems to have treated his parishioners with scorn. He was hated, too, by the officials of the vestry, whom he had accused of corruption. As for John Harrison, the guardian, he was reviled for having chained some of his inmates to the wall, and was later characterised as 'particularly obnoxious to the poor of the neighbourhood'. On the previous Saturday, as a prelude to the imminent violence, his bedroom at Fisher's Buildings had been peppered with gunshot.

Harrison was away on the Monday morning when the mob appeared, but his wife was given notice to quit before nightfall. She is said to have lost no time in evacuating the building with her family through a back window. (The guardian's rooms were at the front, facing the Grange; most of the paupers were accommodated in three thatched out-buildings, since demolished, to the rear.) The mob then set about smashing the place up and setting fire to it. Back at the Vicarage, the rioters told Cobbold that his house would be stormed if their demands – reduced tithes – were not met. They seem to have been egged on by a gathering of the local farmers. Cobbold hurriedly acquiesced, and, having put his name to an agreement, even stood the rioters a quantity of beer from the pub, though he had it duly charged to the poor-book. He would have been aware that the document was worthless, as the tithes were owed not to him but to Magdalen. After three hours in the Plestor the mob dispersed, and devoted the rest of the day to 'eating, drinking and rioting'. On the Tuesday morning, however-er, the rioters, who included men from up to nine neighbouring parishes, set off by a circuitous route to Headley, some seven miles away, and sacked its workhouse. Later, at Kingsley, they destroyed a threshing-machine.

By Thursday, the rioters were being efficiently rounded up by the local magistrates. The prisoners were tried in batches at Winchester in the week before Christmas. Some of the Selborne men were acquitted on a technicality, but others received sentences ranging from hard labour to transportation. They must have been naive – or desperate – to have supposed that their actions would achieve anything but their own ruin.

The leading figure in the disturbances at Selborne was the 37-year-old Robert Holdaway, an unemployed carpenter, wheelwright and hop-planter. Holdaway had migrated to Selborne from Alresford in 1822. He had been the landlord of *The Compasses*, but Cobbold, who thought it disreputable, had lobbied for years to have him dismissed. Having told Holdaway to his face that he would show him 'no mercy', Cobbold had eventually had his way.

Amongst the farmers and labourers of Selborne, Holdaway was regarded as responsible and articulate, and had been their elected spokesman on the day of the riot. An active restraint on the mob, he had striven to put out the fire at the workhouse, and to hold back the mob whilst Cobbold was considering their demands. He had the satisfaction of pointing this out to the Vicar: 'Now, Sir, you once told me you would have no mercy on me. You see I have had mercy on you.' On the Sunday after the riots, following Holdaway's arrest, the pub from which he had been sacked, *The Compasses*, was destroyed by fire. It had no doubt been deliberately set alight, perhaps as an act of revenge. Thanks to the intervention of William Cowburn, a London solicitor who rented The Wakes from the White family, a sentence of death on Holdaway was later commuted. In February 1831, he was instead transported, with four other Selborne men, to New South Wales. None of them ever returned.

Another well-known participant was the 39-year-old labourer and former soldier John Newland, said to be 'a big, strong man, like all the Newlands'. (The 'Newlin' family appear in records here since Tudor times.) Newland lived with his wife and eight children at the top of **Adam's Lane**, at the southern extremity of the village. Normally inoffensive, he was unable to take his drink, having been wounded in the head whilst on active service. A reluctant recruit to the mob, he claimed in court to have been pressed into blowing his horn as it marched down Gracious Street, and later to have been 'knocked down' by some of the other men for showing insufficient enthusiasm. Newland's exploits have been highly romanticised by local legend, which has dubbed him 'The Trumpeter'. He is said to have evaded arrest by holing up on the Hanger, only descending at night-time to receive food from his wife. In reality, Newland had become so insensible with liquor that he had passed out in a field, where he had awoken the following morning 'all wet and chilled'. He had immediately resumed his drinking, had been dragged along with the others to Headley, and remembered nothing more until he had woken up in his own bed on Wednesday with a hangover. It is possible that he then fled to the Hanger and that he spent a couple of nights there; but he had returned to his work by Friday when he was arrested, apparently by Jane Austen's nephew, Edward Knight of Chawton, and was therefore one of the earliest of the rioters to be rounded up.

Newland was sentenced to six months imprisonment with hard labour, which he served in the County Bridewell at Winchester. The more credible part of the legend relates that Ann, his wife, walked during that bitter winter for a day and a night to visit him there, with their six-month-old son William in her arms. The baby's nose became frozen during the ordeal and, ever afterwards, would turn dark blue in cold weather. John Newland, who died in poverty in 1868, at the age of 77, was buried at his family's request beneath the great yew in the church-yard. The so-called 'Trumpeter's Grave' is today marked by a small **granite post**.

As for the hated Cobbold, he refused to give up the parish, where he served for a further eleven years, though he felt it necessary to procure a large mastiff, 'with a neck as thick as a lion's', for protection. Its collar is preserved in a glass cabinet in the North Chancel of the church. Cobbold died in London in 1841, after being knocked down by the Oxford Mail cart at the end of Ludgate Hill. The riots might never have happened at all had he provided better leadership to the village. In the absence of a resident lord of the manor, the impoverished labourers had had nowhere else to turn.

SELECT BIBLIOGRAPHY

Rev. James Anderson, *Saint Mary, Selborne* (4th edition, 1993).

Rev. James Anderson, *The Selborne Yew* (Selborne, 1993).

Rev. James Anderson and Natalie Mees, *A Short Tour of St Mary's Church*, Selborne (1995).

Joseph Bain, 'Sir Adam Gurdun of Selborne', *The Genealogist*, New Series, IV (1887), pp.1–4.

David Burns, 'The Wakes Family', *The Selborne Association Newsletter No.37* (December 1995), pp.16–22.

Calendar of Charters and Documents relating to Selborne and its Priory, ed. W. Dunn Macray (Hampshire Record Society, Winchester, 1891).

Cecil S. Emden, *Gilbert White in his Village* (London, 1956).

Rashleigh Holt-White, *The Life and Letters of Gilbert White of Selborne*, 2 vols. (London, 1901).

Rev. G.E.C. Knapp, 'The Medieval Paving Tiles of the Alton Area of Hampshire', *Proceedings of the Hampshire Field Club and Archaeological Society*, XVIII (1954), pp.295-6.

Deirdre Le Faye, 'Selborne Priory, 1233–1486', *Proceedings of the Hampshire Field Club and Archaeological Society*, XXX (1975), pp.47–71.

Richard Mabey, *Gilbert White: A Biography of the Author of* The Natural History of Selborne (London, 1986).

Natalie Mees, 'Gilbert White's Village in 1999', *The Friends of the Wakes Newsletter No.14* (January 1999), pp.14–20.

Gwyn I. Meirion-Jones, 'The Domestic Buildings of Selborne', *Proceedings of the Hampshire Field Club and Archaeological Society*, XXIX for 1972 (1974).

Gwyn I. Meirion-Jones, 'The Wakes, Selborne: An Architectural Study', *Proceedings of the Hampshire Field Club and Archaeological Society*, XXXIX (1983), pp.145–69.

T.W.E. Roche, *The King of Almayne* (London, 1966).

Anthony Rye, *Gilbert White and his Selborne* (London, 1970).

Walter S. Scott, *White of Selborne and his Times* (London, 1946).

W. Sidney Scott, *A Selborne Handbook* (Selborne, 1950).

Henry C. Shelley, *Gilbert White and Selborne* (London, n.d.).

John Owen Smith, *One Monday in November... The Story of the Selborne and Headley Workhouse Riots of 1830* (Bordon, 1993).

The Victoria County History of Hampshire, ed. W. Page, III (London, 1908), pp.4–16.

Gilbert White, *The Antiquities of Selborne in the County of Southampton*, ed. W. Sidney Scott (London, 1950).

Gilbert White, *The Natural History and Antiquities of Selborne in the County of Southampton*, ed. Thomas Bell, 2 vols. (London, 1877).

Rupert Willoughby, 'Sir Adam de Gurdon and the Pass of Alton', in Barbara Large ed., *The Best of '98: The Eighteenth Annual Writers' Conference* (Winchester, 1998).

E.M. Yates, *Selborne Priory* (Selborne, 1995).

ACKNOWLEDGEMENTS

The author is indebted for their help and encouragement to the Rev. James Anderson, Miss Jean Bowden, Mr Richard Burnip, Dr Michael Clanchy, Mrs Anna Jackson, Mrs Natalie Mees, Mr David Paton, the Earl and Countess of Selborne, Mr and Mrs Peter Stone, Dr E.M. Yates, and above all to Josephine, his incomparable wife and muse, to whom, with love, this work is dedicated.

0953442829

© Rupert Willoughby 2000

Designed by Martin Atcherley and published by the author at
The Old Rectory, Sherborne St John, Hants., RG24 9JD

ISBN 0 9534428 2 9

£4·99